I0159704

Islam Exposed

Islam 101 and what it means to America. Are we in danger? Are Muslims a real threat to our freedom?

By

Floyd C. McElveen

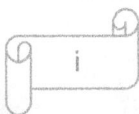

Copyright Page

Author: Floyd C. McElveen
Editor: Greg Bilbo
Cover Illustration, design © 2011   Greg Bilbo
Cover Photos / Unclassified Military Archives & IStockPhoto.com/Joel Carillet

Unless otherwise indicated, Scripture quotations are from:
The Holy Bible, New King James Version © 1984 by Thomas Nelson, Inc.
Other Scripture quotations are from:
The Holy Bible, New International Version (NIV) © 1973, 1984 by International Bible
Society, used by permission of Zondervan Publishing House
New American Standard Bible (NASB) © 1960, 1977 by the Lockman Foundation
The Holy Bible, King James Version (KJV)

Library of Congress Control Number: 2010943482

1. Islamic countries -- Relations -- United States.
2. Terrorism -- Religious aspects – Islam.
3. Islam.
4. Muslims.
5. Islam -- Relations – Christianity.

BISAC / BASIC Classification Suggestions:

1. REL037000RELIGION / Islam / General
2. POL037000POLITICAL SCIENCE / Political Freedom & Security
/ Terrorism
3. POL004000POLITICAL SCIENCE / Political Freedom & Security / Civil Rights

ISBN-13: 978-0-9831983-0-7   V 1.1

Big Mac Publishers / Sylacauga, Alabama 35151
Printed and bound in the United States of America

Islam Exposed

▶ ▶ ▶ ▶ ▶ An incredibly compact, informative book providing the basics of their faith, the truth about Islam and its deadly mission worldwide, with alarming eye-popping documented revelations concerning the real Muslim agenda and the imminent threat to America. *Powerful!!—**The Publisher***

▶ ▶ ▶ ▶ ▶ At the dawn of the new millennium, the world is being confronted with an absolute culture of hate, characterized by paroxysms of international terrorism against civilians, and religious intolerance. This culture of hate has multiple heads from Algeria to Afghanistan, to Indonesia, via Gaza and the West Bank, Damascus, Cairo, Khartoum, Teheran, and Karachi. It scatters the seeds of terrorism from one end of the earth to the other.

This hate, which suppresses freedom of thought and condemns difference, calls itself "Islamic Jihad." It draws on religious texts whose interpretation other Muslims dispute. Moreover, because these moderate Muslims challenge this interpretation of Jihad, wishing to live in peace with the non-Muslim peoples and nations of the world, their lives are threatened. There is constant bloodshed in Algeria. Jihad is disseminating death and terror in Israel. In Southern Sudan, **Jihad has caused the death of some two million people**, generated an even larger number of refugees, lead to the enslavement of tens of thousands, and produced deadly famines.

In Indonesia, some **200,000** deaths resulted from Jihad violence in East Timor. Christians have been pursued and massacred, and their churches burned down by Jihadists in the Moluccas and other Indonesian islands. The death toll in these violent attacks is over **10,000**, while an additional **8,000** Christians have been forcibly converted to Islam, including many who were circumcised. Atrocities are also being committed by Jihadists in both the Philippines and some northern Nigerian states. Hundreds of innocent people died when Jihad struck at the Jewish Community Center of Buenos Aires in Argentina, and the U.S. embassies in Kenya and Tanzania. In Egypt, Jihadists have massacred Copts in their churches and villages, and murdered European tourists. Christians in Pakistan and in Iran live in terror of accusations of blasphemy, which, if "proven," can yield a death sentence. And a cataclysmic act of Jihad terror resulted in the slaughter of nearly **3,000** innocent civilians of multiple faiths and nationalities in New York, on September 11, 2001. None of these victims were guilty of any crime. They were murdered and mutilated out of hate.

Bat Yeor - - http://www.papillonsartpalace.com/cultuHre.htm

Reviews

Islamic Terrorists, "Jihadist," are clearly a raging destructive infection around the world that will not stop until eliminated with a world-class *antibiotic* … This is as large an issue as two colliding cultures, which will spread more violence onto American soil, if American doesn't change its behavior in various ways and regain God's pleasure. We have taken off our spiritual armor and are now witnessing the predictable results which may suddenly spread horrifically and uncontrollably across America. -- *Retired Military Colonel*

Eye opener! Yes, it was. It was timely for me, especially the part about the "Growth of Islam!" -- *Gladys Breckenridge from Canada*

I have taken well-armed clients into the wilderness in Alaska for many years from our lodge on the Holitna River. I am here to tell you that wild animals have a far better chance of surviving than our American way of life does. We are dead in the center of the sights of supremely powerful weapons poised and ready and held by terrorists bent on our destruction.

Rockstar, Author, (Wild Men, Wild Alaska II) Big Game Guide, www.alaskan-adventures.com

When was the last time a terrorist attack anywhere was by a *non-Muslim*? Very rare! *Think about it.*

Dedication

I thank my family for their love and faithfulness. All my children, now grown, love the Lord, and I love them. But primarily, I want to thank Virginia, my precious dear wife of 62 years. She went to be with Jesus in July 2010. She had always wanted to meet Jesus and died with the sure knowledge that she would be in his arms the moment she left this earth.

What amazing hope we have in Christ. She died without fear and was thrilled that she would finally meet her Blessed Savior. She never wavered in her faith and proved that right up to her last breath, dying peacefully, with a smile on her face and joy in her heart.

She lived a life that reflected God's love. It was a love that flowed through her for all, regardless of race, status or anything else. Everyone who met her was touched by her humility and love. I learned more from her than she ever learned from me. I miss her. I can't wait to see her again.

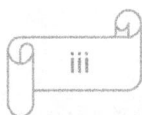

Introduction

It is the hope that Virginia had that I want to share. This hope is facing great peril in the free world.

Unfortunately, all religions do not lead to God. None do in fact, of themselves. The only way to God is through his Son, Jesus, whatever your denomination. This is a message certain groups are trying to stifle, and going to great lengths to do so.

I want Americans to realize the precarious ledge of freedom we are slipping from and reach out in part to open-minded Muslims, if they exist.

Do we comprehend the track our "freedom train" is barreling down? Will we continue to stand idly by while everything we cherish as a free nation is taken from us—including freedom of religion? Christians are dying worldwide—at the hands of Muslims. All Muslim nations treat Christians as 2nd class citizens and **none** give Christians equal rights Christian nations give them.

March 18, 2011 - Crosswalk.com

LAHORE, Pakistan (CDN) — "A Christian serving a life sentence in Karachi Central Jail on accusations that he had sent text messages blaspheming the prophet of Islam died Tuesday amid suspicions that he was murdered."

Note: Blasphemy, *punishable by death* to **criticize** Islam! Muslims cleverly use this device of being "offended" to mislead and initiate the basics of Sharia Law. Read on!

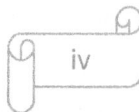

Table of Contents

Table of Contents

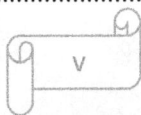

PAKISTAN

THOUSANDS RALLY FOR BLASPHEMY LAW

Man who killed critic of the law earns praise

BY ASHRAF KHAN
The Associated Press

KARACHI, PAKISTAN • Tens of thousands of demonstrators marched in Pakistan's largest city on Sunday to oppose any change to national blasphemy laws and to praise a man charged with murdering a provincial governor who had

WHY WE CARE

Pakistan is a crucial, but tenuous, U.S. ally in the war on terrorism, and officials worry that increasingly militant Islamists could send the country over a tipping point. Many U.S. officials believe Pakistan isn't aggressive enough in fighting terrorism and is still a haven for jihadists.

campaigned against the divisive legislation.

The rally of up to 50,000 people in downtown Karachi was one of the largest

demonstrations of support for the laws, which make insulting Islam a capital offense. It was organized before the governor of

Punjab province, Salman Taseer, was shot dead on Tuesday in Islamabad by a bodyguard who told a court he considered Taseer a blasphemer.

Muslim groups have praised the bodyguard, Mumtaz Qadri, and have used Taseer's death to warn others not to speak out against the much-derided

SEE PAKISTAN • PAGE 2

PAKISTAN: Blasphemy law ignites bitter debate

FROM PAGE 1

laws.

The size of the Karachi rally, which was large even by the standards of the city of 16 million, showed how bitter the argument is over the decades-old laws.

Although courts typically overturn blasphemy convictions and no executions have been carried out, rights activists say the laws are used to settle rivalries and persecute religious minorities.

Amid the threats from groups defending the law, the prime minister ruled out any changes to the legislation on Sunday, even as one of his key Cabinet ministers promised reforms were still on the agenda.

"This huge rally today has categorically signaled that nobody could dare to amend the blasphemy law," said Fazlur Rehman, the key speaker at Sunday's demonstration and head of the Taliban-linked conservative religious party Jamiat Ulema Islam.

He said Taseer "was responsible for his own murder" because he had criticized the law.

The laws came under renewed international scrutiny late last year when a 45-year-old Christian woman, Asia Bibi, was sentenced to death for allegedly insulting Islam's prophet.

People accused of blasphemy are often killed by extremists or spend significant amounts of time behind bars.

In some cases, the charges border on the ridiculous: A man was recently held because he threw away a

business card of someone whose first name is Muhammad.

The Karachi rally represented all major Muslim groups and sects in Pakistan's most populous city and was one of the few to bring together moderate and conservative Muslims.

Police officer Irshad Sehar estimated 40,000 to 50,000 people attended.

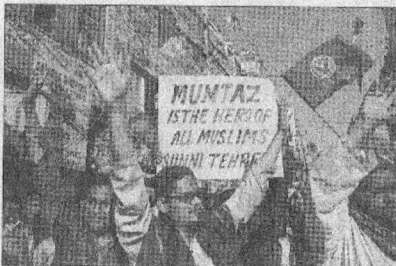

Supporters of Pakistani religious party Sunni Tehreek rallied Sunday in support of Mumtaz Qadri, accused of killing Punjab governor Salman Taseer.

THE ASSOCIATED PRESS

*Note: In this 1/10/2011 article: A man is **praised** for murdering someone who simply criticized Muslim law!*

Islam Exposed!

Myth #1 – Islam is a Peaceful Religion.

Millions of Americans, some of them Christians, believe that Mohammad, who worshipped the Moon God of the Quraysh tribe in Mecca, as still seen in the Crescent Moon on Muslim banners, founded a peaceful religion. This is the dogma we hear continually from our leftist media and out-of-touch academia. Well quite simply, this is absolutely false.

Consider carefully this alarming statement (paraphrased) along with other information throughout the book from www.bibleprobe.com:

When a Muslim or the media declare that Islam is a religion of peace, they are either ignorant of the Koran (Qur'an), or are deceitfully twisting the real meaning of "peace," since the "peace" they refer to extends only to those within the Muslim Community. The deceit is that they (Muslims) will not explain or tell you exactly what they mean, yet their own writings make it very clear.

According to the Qur'an: "Muhammad is the Apostle of Allah and his final prophet. Those who follow him are merciful to one another, but ruthless to unbelievers" (Sura 48:29).

"Kill the Mushrikun (unbelievers) wherever you find them, and capture them and besiege them, and lie in wait for them in each and every bush . . ." (Sura 9:5).

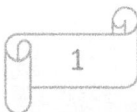

Also see (Sura 9:29) PICKTHAL: "Fight against such of those who have been given the Scripture (Christians and Jews) as believe not in Allah nor the Last Day, and forbid not that which Allah hath forbidden by His messenger, and follow not the Religion of Truth, until they pay the tribute readily, being brought low."

Another statement which also quotes Muslim holy writings (Sura 47:4):

"Fa'idhā Laqītumu Al-Ladhīna Kafarū Faḍarba Ar-Riqābi attaá 'Idhā 'Athkhantumūhum Fashuddū Al-Wathāqa Fa'immā Mannāan Ba`du Wa 'Immā Fidā'an Ĥattaá Taḍa`a Al-Ĥarbu 'Awzārahā Dhālika Wa Law Yashā'u Allāhu Lāntaşara Minhum Wa Lakin Liyabluwa Ba`ḍakum Biba`ḍin Wa Al-Ladhīna Qutilū Fī Sabīli Allāhi Falan Yuḍilla 'A`mālahum."

It means: Therefore, WHEN YOU MEET THE UNBELIEVERS, SMITE AT THEIR NECKS at length, when ye have thoroughly subdued them, bind a bond firmly (on them): thereafter (is the time for) either generosity or ransom: Until the war lays down its burdens. Thus (are ye commanded): but if it had been Allah's Will, He could certainly have exacted retribution from them (Himself); but (He lets you fight) in order to test you, some with others. But those who are slain in the Way of Allah, He will never let their deeds be lost.

Many Qur'an translators have tried to soften the meaning in their translation by adding the words "in war" in brackets after the word "Unbelievers" but they are NOT there in the original Arabic text. Modifying "holy" writings is a common ploy Muslims use to deceive and cover up the facts of their beliefs. Read the earliest texts and manuscripts whenever possible to know the truth.

Islam is NOT a peaceful religion passively content to co-exist with other religions. Both Muslim holy books (Qur'an/Koran and Hadith) contain commands for Muslims to subjugate the world, militarily. Muhammad commanded Muslims to spread Islam through *Offensive* Jihad; the conquest of non-Muslim lands. Muslims are commanded to take back land that was formerly Muslim, such as Israel. These are not idle threats.

Consider this: Almost all terrorist organizations worldwide are connected with Muslim organizations. Mohammad, their primary prophet (who never prophesied by the way) led 27 campaigns against innocent people, caravans and villages, looting and killing thousands. And he planned 38 more that never materialized. He states in the Hadith, "I am the prophet that laughs when killing my enemies." Some of these killings were amazingly brutal.

Mohammad is the Muslim leader. He is the heart and soul of their philosophy. Such killings are occurring worldwide today. We saw a horrible example of this on 9/11. And Muslims universally rejoiced and celebrated then and continue to do so on its anniversary each year since.

Christian and Jewish martyrs say, "**I** will die for what I believe." Muslim suicide bombers and martyrs say, "**You** will die for what I believe."

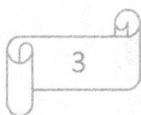

Growth of Islam

Incidentally, being a Muslim is not specifically an Arab phenomenon. Estimates are that 85% of Muslims are *non-Arabic*, as seen in the Soviet Union and Indonesia. Why? In the past 50 years Islam has grown 500% and is the world's fastest growing religion, while Christianity has grown 47%, and less than 10% the pace of Islam.

England, France and Europe are fast becoming Muslim. So are Mexico, Canada, Cuba, Venezuela, and other Central and South American countries. Fidel Castro and Hugo Chavez are deeply involved with and honored by Muslim leaders.

Our once dearly beloved Canada is now for all practical purposes a Muslim country, with a huge Muslim buildup in Toronto, where Muslims from around the world come to train others or to be trained and implement Jihad and Sharia law.

Astonishingly, 225 cross-border roads from Canada to the US are left unguarded. Cruelty unspeakable is just around the corner.

How did this all happen? Well, one reason is our own "tolerance" attitudes in the West. That "tolerance" needs a face lift. It is used against us. We should not tolerate that which destroys.

Consider this. Islam is very tempting to non-Christian men. Men have absolute power in Islam. Wives and children must submit. Men can have temporary marriages and multiple wives. They can abuse their women indiscriminately and without retribution. They can kill. Strong violent men love this. And violent nations love it too. Why aren't women screaming bloody murder?

Another reason is money and lots of it. Arabs have poured millions of dollars into very specific areas of the US and Canada. They donate hundreds of millions to prestigious colleges. Their own professors weave the deceit of Islam on beguiled students. Students that graduate and go on to unwittingly or maybe knowingly advance the cause of Sharia law and Islam in insidious ways politically, in education and in religious circles.

Muslims donate heavily to political candidates and causes. Much of this is done on the sly to keep sources hidden. The oil of the Islamic nations has enriched and empowered Muslims to buy their way into countless countries worldwide. America isn't immune. I won't delve into specifics but some of the highest reaches of government have benefited greatly from these "donations."

There is info in a book by Moody Adams, "The Religion that is Raping America" that should astonish African-Americans. Moody writes that according to African Historian J.E. Inikori, Arab/Muslims were deeply involved as major slave traders (pg. 57). From 1650 to 1900, black Africa lost 14.4 million people to the slave trade. Yet many blacks today are drawn to the Muslim faith.

This is a mystery to me. There were whites in the slave trade as well and they are rightfully castigated

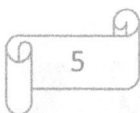

for their awful deeds, but they were not alone. Muslims were the primary players in the slave trade. Where is this in the history books?

I still cringe when I see the results of the Muslim taking of Sudan, with thousands of naked and half-naked men, women and children fleeing for their lives; starving and terrified, with no help or hope, and being slaughtered mercilessly. One of my friends slipped in and took pictures of the horror of Muslim genocide on "unbelievers" as Muslims enforced Jihad and Sharia law.

As the www.bibleprobe.com website states: Islam works in much the same way as satanically-inspired communism, which is by subversive means. Islam has spread worldwide since its inception mostly by the sword and intimidation.

Muslims actually call themselves "Din e-Sif," or *religion of the sword*. Islamic Laws are very clear—Jews and Christians have no rights whatsoever to independent existence. They can live under Islamic Rule provided they keep to the rules that Islam promulgates for them. This method of conversion by the sword, intimidation and fear is one of the most convincing proofs that Islam is a purely human invention.

Concomitantly, it is precisely the fact that Christianity prevailed against all the forces and powers in the world out to destroy it, by merely the force of its truth, that points to the superhuman origin of Christianity.

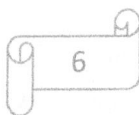

If present trends continue, the USA is on track to be a Muslim Nation between 2021 and 2035, perhaps sooner. The Muslims have now taken dead aim at Israel and America. They enlist suicide bombers and terrorist groups like Al-Qaeda, Hezbollah, Hamas, and many other terrorist organizations, to get the world to submit to Islam, whose very name ironically means "submission."

History of Islam

There are many sources to learn more about the specific history of Islam. Suffice it to say, it is a very fractured process, parallel manuscripts, and no cohesive consistent methodology.

There are literally countless contradictions in early manuscripts and most have been shielded or changed to hide the lack of credibility. Naturally Muslims dispute this but it doesn't take much research to discover the truth. Most were written 150 to 300 years after the events and many were from scraps of paper, traditions passed down from memory and from various disconnected groups or leaders such as Caliphs or Clerics, usually to make up rules or laws to control their fiefdoms. The documentation is suspect, sparse and garners little credibility from truly neutral experts.

The Koran / Qur'an

The Qur'an, aside from its threats, is filled with false claims and ill-based assumptions. It states that Allah, the Moon God, is the only real God, Islam the

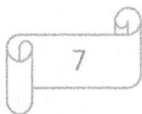

only true religion, and of course denies the Trinity/Godhead (God, the Holy Spirit and Jesus as one) and dismisses Jesus as being the only way to Heaven.

The Koran claims Abraham's father was Azar, but the Bible says it was Terah. According to the Koran, Abraham lived and worshipped in Mecca. The Bible states Hebron. In the Koran, Abraham planned to sacrifice Ishmael but the Bible clearly indicates Isaac was the sacrificial son.

Abraham did not build the Kabah, as the Koran says. One of the strangest claims by the Koran, (Suras 21, 68, 69, and 9:69) is that Abraham was thrown into a fire by Nimrod. Of course this is impossible. Nimrod lived centuries before Abraham. The Koran claims that Mary, the human Mother of Jesus, was the *sister* of Moses and Aaron, and gave birth to Jesus under a palm tree. These are but a few of many false and curious statements in the Koran.

So how about evidence from science? According to the Muslim Holy books, the sun sets in a muddy bog (Qur'an: 18:86).

www.bibleprobe.com summarizes it well:

Question: How can the Qur'an be trusted when it contains numerous "*divinely inspired*" contradictions? If God has a history of abrogating (changing) his own revelations as is done in the Qur'an, then how can we be certain he will not abrogate it again in the future? If Allah can abrogate his eternal speech, how can you trust him with your eternal soul?

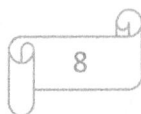

The Hadith

The other supposedly "inspired" book of the Muslims, the Hadith, was collected 150 years after the death of Mohammad. It was gleaned from thousands of sayings and actions of Mohammad and written in part on leaves and bark.

Insanely, Mohammad taught that if urine got on an individual, they would go to Hell, so he gave specific rules about how, where, and in what way to urinate. Can you imagine how difficult that would be— impossible for an infant or anyone else!

Also, according to the Hadith, Mohammad was superstitious. When he had to urinate or defecate, he was afraid evil spirits might enter his body so he prayed for special protection (Morey's book, pg. 203-204, Hadith vol. 1, ch. 57, no. 2151).

According to the Hadith, Jihad, or Holy War, was significant to Mohammad. He made it the second most important deed in Islam. Moreover, the Hadith opens up the possibility that those killed as suicide bombers or fighting in Jihad, could get 72 perpetual virgins in Allah's Paradise (Morey's book, pg. 76-88, 117-174, 177-208).

Nasikh

The Muslim religious leaders, the Caliphs or Clerics, have developed a major evasive philosophy, which protects their religious books, and their religion, called Naskh, as Mark Gabriel explains in his book (pg. 228). It is a clever device. A verse can now simply be

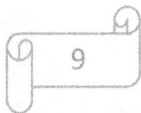

rendered obsolete or useless, by an added verse which is inserted in its place, or even if the verse remains in the Koran.

Thus they can hide or "render" any verse or verses which might be embarrassing to them, unexplainable in their "inspired" books, or awkward in the Muslim religion, essentially making that verse or verses "of no effect." This is disingenuous, satanic, and a devilish master stroke. This is spin that is accepted by a gullible following. When Naskh is used, it is then called Nasikh.

Mohammad

Robert Morey is a Christian apologist and pastor who has written a number of books and pamphlets. He is the founder of the California Biblical University and Seminary. He has diligently done his homework and research on this topic. Naturally he has received scrutiny and criticism from the groups he exposes.

Morey outlines the origin of the Muslim religion which initially was formed from the 360 false gods in the Kabah at Mecca. Allah actually translates as "Moon God" ("Islamic Invasion," pg. 19 and following).

When Mohammad discovered that Jews and Christians refused his religion, he ceased to bow toward Jerusalem, and bowed toward Mecca instead. He began to raid, plunder and kill the "people of the book," Jews and Christians.

At one time, Mohammad beheaded hundreds of those who surrendered (Dave Hunt, "Judgment Day, the Battle of Badr," pg. 113-117). Dave Hunt's book does a superb job of showing clearly that current events are undeniably fulfilling Biblical prophecy of the last days, particularly concerning the Muslim threat, and the eagerly anticipated coming of the Lord Jesus Christ.

Hunt's book, "A Cup of Trembling," also furnishes a mass of valuable information on Muslims, Jerusalem, and the future of Israel.

The Muslim religion began in 610 A.D. It has grown exponentially. The Sunnis (part of the more conservative faction and usually believed to be less violent, not peaceful necessarily, just less violent) number close to 90%. The Shiites (the more radical and violent faction) consist of about 10% of this billion-plus Islamic religion, with a few million mystic Sufis included. The Sunnis and the Shiites have fought bloody wars against each other for hundreds of years. They are however, united when dealing with non-Muslims.

Two "inspired books" motivate all Muslims, the Koran/Qur'an and the Hadith. Muslims believe in, adhere to and use (Sura 9:5, 9:3, and 9:29), which command devout Muslims to kill all non-believers (non-Muslims). The more devout a Muslim, the more dangerous he is, and all Muslims at bottom are devout, even so-called "moderates."

At age 25, Mohammad married a rich woman named Khadija, who was 40 years old. She was creative and promoted his seizures and visions as being from God (Morey, pg. 86-87). Mohammad was also a pedophile, "Marrying a total of 16 women, including a 6 or 7 year old child named Aesha, with whom the marriage was consummated when she was a 9 years old. Twenty-four lived with Mohammad, including Mary, a Christian, who remained a slave rather than have any sexual involvement with Mohammad" (Morey, pg. 86).

No Muslims can rightly leave their religion; if they do, they might be killed. Dr. Mark Gabriel, professor at Al-Azhar, the leading, oldest and most prestigious Muslim Seminary in the world in Cairo, Egypt, tells of torture, a bloody stabbing, and even worse, because he merely *questioned* Islam.

His own father tried to kill him (Mark Gabriel, *not his real name*, "Islam and Terrorism," pg. 1-32). Some Christians gave him a Bible. Their love and the truth brought him to Jesus.

Jesus, the Son of God, God the Son, declared in John 14:6, Jesus said unto him, "*I am the way, the truth, and the life, no man cometh unto the Father but by me.*"

Jesus shed His blood on the cross to save all who would come to Him, and believe in His death, shed blood, burial and resurrection for them. This includes me, you, and everyone. Surrender to Him; believe in Him with all your heart; call on Him for salvation—and be saved. Or deny Him and spend eternity in Hell. It is just that stark (Romans 10:9, 10-13, 1 John 5:13).

Muslims do not believe that Jesus himself was crucified, but rather an imposter somehow died on the cross. And of course they do not believe Jesus rose from the grave.

Holy War

Jihad among other things, is a Holy War on all "unbelievers," especially "people of the book," (Jews and Christians) but also all non-Muslims.

The word "Jihad" actually stems from the Arabic root word J-H-D. That word means "to strive." Islam's ultimate goal is to literally eradicate all other religions except Islam. Muhammad encouraged his followers to spread Islam by force. This is contrary to Christianity's goal of spreading the good news Gospel of Jesus throughout the world so that all have an opportunity to *accept* or *reject* God's offer of forgiveness.

In Islam, there are 5 types of Jihad. *All 5 are obligatory for every Muslim*. They are:

1. Jihad al-nafs. This is the striving against one's inner self.

2. Jihad al-Shaitan. This is striving against Satan.

3. Jihad al-munafiqeen. This is striving against the hypocrites.

4. Jihad al-faasiqeen. This is striving against corrupt Muslims.

5. Jihad al-kuffaar. This is striving against the disbelievers (of Muhammad and/or Allah).

There is a 6th Jihad converted Muslims speak of (search youtube.com). It is "Cultural Jihad" and involves using sly and clever means to undermine America and Western Cultures. Muslims train gifted students and send them to America with specific tasks. the Washington Examiner Online reports: "Radical Islam is coming to America in subtle, sophisticated ways as part of a cultural jihad set up to undermine democratic traditions from within and to make way for a new theocratic state in the U.S."

http://washingtonexaminer.com/blogs/examiner-opinion-zone/2009/05/documentary-warns-against-cultural-jihad-operating-within-us#ixzz1HGNI3G3Z

"Stealth Jihad," by Robert Spencer outlines how insidious these methods are. American Muslims are even fostering "Sharia law" in grade school lunches and many other innocuous programs and places. They are building a groundwork tradition that will allow them to move into more serious areas. Basically anything that "offends" them is distilled down to a religious issue and thus forced on naïve groups that fail to see the danger.

Muslims believe "Sharia" law, must be imposed worldwide. Under this horrible law, women are second class citizens in Saudi Arabia. And the killings on 9/11, towers full of thousands of innocent men, women and children dying in a fiery bloodbath, are not *condemned*, but CELEBRATED!

This may seem shocking to us, but the following is but one of the raids Mohammad led his men on during a time when he was developing this idea of "Holy War" and "Jihad." This was not divinely inspired. It was a way to take "booty" and repay enemies. *Islam* was a religious tool and his "revelations" a device to empower his way of life and establish control. This is not a new tactic.

Date: March (Ramadan) 17, 623 A.D.

Place: The well of Badr. Victims: 70 merchants from Quraysh Tribe of Mecca, 200 from the Quraysh army which came to defend them.

The merchandise being carried by this caravan was worth more than 50,000 Gold Dinars. Muhammad ganged up all the criminals of Medina and set out to raid the caravan with 300 men. The Meccans got word of the raid and sent out an army to protect the caravan. Throughout the entire battle, Mohammad cowered in a hut which his men made for him. There he cried and prayed with feverish anxiety. At one point he came out of the hut and threw pebbles in the enemy's direction, screaming "Let evil look on your faces!" and "By him who holds my soul in his hands, anyone who fights for me today will go to paradise!"

The Muslims killed over two hundred and took seventy prisoners. All seventy of the prisoners were ransomed, but any prisoner who did not fetch a ransom had his head chopped off and tossed into a pit. Muhammad was gratified at the sight of his murdered victims.

After the battle, he sent his followers to look for the corpse of Abu Jahal, one of the Meccans who had criticized him openly. When his corpse was found, they cut off the head and threw it down at Muhammad's feet.

The *Apostle of peace* cried out in delirious joy, "Rejoice! Here lies the head of the enemy of Allah!

Praise Allah, for there is no other but he! It is more acceptable to me than the choicest camel in all Arabia."

The Prophet had ordered a great pit to be dug for the bodies of the innocents to be dumped. The Muslims proceeded to hack the corpse's limbs into pieces. As the bloodied mass of bodies was being thrown into the pit, a feverishly excited Muhammad screamed, "O People of the Pit, have you found that what Allah threatened is true now? For I have found that what my Lord promised was true! Rejoice All Muslims!"

One prisoner taken was the defiant Al Nadr Ibn al Harith, who had earlier taken Muhammad's challenge of telling better stories than him. Muhammad ordered Nadr's head cut off in his presence, so he could exult in the pleasure of beheading the man who had insulted him.

Another prisoner, Uqba ibn Abi Muait (aka: Ocba) was decapitated in front of the Prophet. Before being killed the prisoner cried out pitifully "O Prophet, who will look after my children if I should die?" *The Great Prophet of the Religion of Peace* coldly spat out "Hellfire," as the blade came down and spattered his clothes with Uqba's blood.

Muhammad continued by saying, "Wretch that thou wast! And persecutor! Unbeliever in God, in his Prophet, and in his Book. I give thanks unto the Lord that hath slain thee, and comforted mine eyes thereby."

Naturally Muhammad needed a revelation that would not only absolve him of all the guilt for murdering so many innocent people, but also give him the "divine right" to get a huge share of the plundered booty. Quite a few revelations magically appeared after the battle of Badr.

This great booty became a bone of contention between Muhammad and his band of thieves. Like always, when it favored Muhammad--he soon received a revelation from Allah shown in the eighth Chapter of the Qur'an, titled Al-Anfal, "The Spoils of War," or "Booty," warning Muslims not to consider booty won at Badr to belong to anyone except Muhammad. Ultimately Muhammad distributed this booty and kept a fifth for himself.

His revelation? "They ask thee concerning things taken as spoils of war? Say, (*Such spoils are at the disposal of Allah and the Messenger Muhammad*) so fear Allah, and keep straight the relations between yourselves. Obey Allah and his Messenger, if ye do believe." (Qur'an 8:1)

This successful battle, and its great booty, after years of failure and military loses (including the Battle of Uhud in 625 AD, where the Muslims and Muhammad were routed) launched Muhammad as a military force. When men saw the great booty that could be gained by following Muhammad they began arriving in droves.

Certain "rules of war" (doctrines of Islam) were also developed by Muhammad after this Battle. Bloody vengeance against one's enemies belongs not solely to the Lord, but also to those who submit to him on earth. From this we get the real meaning of Islam: "Submission." *Those who reject Islam are "the vilest of creatures" and thus deserve no mercy* (Qur'an 98:6). *Therefore, when ye meet the Unbelievers, smite at their necks.* (**Holy War** info to here reference: www.bibleprobe.com).

We can hide our heads in the sand and pretend these patterns don't still exist or we can see how Muslims have been indoctrinated from infancy and begin to understand that they believe in a far different way than we can even imagine.

Don't believe this is relevant today? Here is an article by Ken Blackwell Dec 15, 2010, published online at WorldMag.com. *The Persecution of Christians in the 'Muslim' world.*

The New York Times ran a front-page article on Christian persecution in Iraq, noting, "A new wave of Iraqi Christians has fled to northern Iraq or abroad amid a campaign of violence against them and growing fear that the country's security forces are unable or, more ominously, unwilling to protect them."

The **Times** goes on to inform us that "more than half of Iraq's Christian community, estimated to number 800,000 to 1.4 million before the American-led invasion in 2003, have already left the country."

What is the administration doing to put pressure on the al-Maliki government in Baghdad to stop these murders of Christians? We have heard endlessly of this administration's "outreach to the Muslim world."

That term—"Muslim world"—may itself be part of the problem. By telling Shia and Sunni Muslims that the Middle East is their world, are we not saying that Middle Eastern Christians and Jews don't belong there?

The Christian community in Iraq has been there since the beginnings of the Church. Bible readers will recognize Nineveh Province, one of the regions in modern-day Iraq. Didn't some biblical character named Jonah have a rendezvous with destiny there? The Chaldean Assyrian Christians—note their Bible name— speak Aramaic, which is the language scholars tell us Jesus spoke. Yet these people, too, are being driven away.

The Wall Street Journal also has taken up the cause of Christian persecution and has done so eloquently:

"With the rise of radical Islam, this tradition of peaceful and productive coexistence has been displaced by a practice of religious cleansing. It is estimated that of the 100,000 Christians who once lived in Mosul, Iraq, only 5,000 remain. In Egypt, Coptic Christians have been brutalized. Assaults on churches increase around Easter or Christmas, as worshipers attempt to observe holy days."

Where is the U.S. State Department on all of this? Where is the White House press office?

By constantly bowing to the idea of a "Muslim world," the Obama administration undercuts its own professed desire for peace in the region. When was the last time we heard anyone speak of "Christendom?"

The President recently compared his Republican opponents on Capitol Hill to "hostage takers." Are they Shia? Sunni? Could he list the number of non-Muslim hostage takers the world has witnessed in the past 40 years?

Both Iraq and Afghanistan have constitutions that the United States helped them craft following the U.S.-led invasions of their countries. Our own State Department advisers insisted on including in these post-Saddam and post-Taliban constitutions something strange called "repugnancy clauses."

These repugnancy clauses say, in sum, that notwithstanding anything else in this constitution, nothing may be done by this government that is repugnant to Islam. Who gets to determine what is repugnant to Islam? Who has historically determined repugnancy? Is it not the mullahs? And which mullahs might that be? Why, the mullahs with more guns, of course.

By insisting on these repugnancy clauses, our own State Department advisers have constitutionalized ethnic and religious strife. Not only are Christians and Jews in mortal peril in the affected countries, we see that off-brand Muslims are in danger, too. If you are a Shia in a Sunni-dominant country, like Saudi Arabia, you can expect to be jailed.

If you are a Sunni in Iran, you're likewise in trouble. And, of course, if you're a Sufi in any Muslim-dominant country, heaven help you.

Our nameless State Department types—those who insisted on and got these repugnancy clauses—also ignored our own American contribution to religious liberty. Thomas Jefferson was our first secretary of State. His closest friend, James Madison, served as secretary of State for 8 years in President Jefferson's Cabinet. They knew something about diplomacy, as well as being among America's greatest advocates for religious freedom.

When they collaborated on the Virginia Statute for Religious Freedom, they laid the foundation for civil liberty in a constitutional republic. It is axiomatic that if you murder your neighbor because he worships differently than you do, you will never enjoy democracy. Why don't our State Department functionaries understand this?

It does not matter how many millions of purple-fingered voters approved these fatally flawed constitutions. If those same voters go to the polls and elect politicians who refuse to protect the lives of Christians in their midst, it is all for naught.

"I expect that a month from now not a single Christian will be left in Mosul," the *Times* reports Nelson P. Khoshaba as saying. Khoshaba is an engineer who worked in the Iraqi city's waterworks. Is he not just the kind of educated citizen that Iraq needs in its post-Saddam era? But if Khoshaba and his family must flee their historic homeland, what does this say about our enterprise in Iraq?

Wasn't there something we read in dispatches from our Pentagon about "Operation Iraqi Freedom?" What freedom is this? Freedom to flee? Why have the Secretary of State and President been deaf to the cries of persecuted Christians? Why don't they seem to care?

The Crusades

The Crusades, led by Pope Urban II, was a Catholic so-called "Christian" war with seven campaigns, four of which were major. This monolithic massacre occurred 1095-1291. It was brutal and bloody, *with Jews and Christians and others slaughtered*, along with Muslims, particularly the Turkish or Kurdish brand.

This whole period has been deceitfully presented as "Christians" murdering Muslims. This is not the whole story. Real Christians were killed and persecuted right along with Muslims. The Crusades began in part because of the killings and torture of Christians in Jerusalem by Muslims.

Pilgrimages to Jerusalem, once permitted by the Muslims, were forbidden when the Muslim Turks took over Jerusalem. The Ottoman Empire was drenched in unmitigated atrocities and gore. The ferocity of the most intense battles was from 1299 to 1453, when mighty and formerly impregnable Constantinople fell into Muslim hands. They conquered the world of their day, from France to China for Islam.

I do not condone many of the atrocities of the Crusades, but I do understand their initial purpose and that the whole truth has been revised a good deal. But the distant past is not an excuse to brutalize the Western world even if all of the grievances were true. Instead, this is just another device to spread hatred of Christians among Muslims and promote the cause of Islam.

Sharia Law

Myth #2 – Sharia Law = Religious Policy.

Sharia law is not religious law but a political and social force to rule individuals. It is a method of control for Muslim religious leaders in every aspect of a Muslim's life. This cannot be stressed enough. Men rule. It is a total social system of domination of the fabric of human life from cradle to grave. This law eliminates all freedom as we know it.

Much of it is based on spiritual tradition, the Qur'an and Hadith, just as our constitution and conventional laws have their basis on the Bible and Ten Commandments; however neither are our laws "religious" laws. This fallacy must be understood. It is at the heart of how Muslims gain control, especially in "religious tolerant" societies like us who go way overboard to accommodate.

In fact, each of our states and cities has various laws governing the people of that region and all the laws in our nation have similar foundations, but do differ amongst localities. This is exactly what we find under the so-called Sharia law. Different localities, tribes, regions and so forth have various rules and regulations, loosely based on an overall theme, just like most nations.

Under Sharia law, in Saudi Arabia, women are not allowed to drive a car, must wear a veil and long dark robes, and can be beaten to death by their husbands if they even speak to another man when their husband is not present; conversely, a man can have 4 wives.

I can cite many examples of extreme bias, especially toward women in regions where Sharia law reigns. But the bottom line is that those in power use Sharia law to control their subjects. It is political anarchy. It has little to do with compassion, human rights or what is best for society as a whole. It has to do with a rigid patriarchal society that rules with an iron fist. Men reign supreme under Sharia law.

One of the primary reasons we fought the War of Emancipation from England was for "religious freedom." We did not want the Church ruling our lives, and we made it very clear in our constitution that there was to be a separation of Church and State.

The Church of England was governed by corrupt bishops who wielded absolute power. Absolute power corrupts. Excommunication was a real threat and subjects were terrified of this ultimate punishment and banishment. It was feared to be a path to hell.

Muslims do the same things. Banishment and death are the norm. And Muslims have ZERO tolerance under Sharia law. Quite a contrast from our constitution and current way of life.

While our noble and brave soldiers fought to save Kuwait and Saudi Arabia in Desert Storm, they were forbidden to read Bibles openly, or *publically* practice Christianity. One-way tolerance doesn't work.

Sharia Law in Practice

Under the guise of "religious freedom," Muslims have been worming their way into our society and courts. Rulings are starting to slant toward "tolerating" Sharia law in various communities by falsely viewing these "rules and beliefs" as religious mandates and culture (thus must be tolerated) rather than seeing them for what they are. They are actually counterproductive laws to our own Christian-based laws. It has nothing to do with religion, but is all about control.

In the case of Christian Scientist, the courts have understood this disparity and ruled against them when their rules conflict with the state. The media and courts seem not to understand that Sharia law is in this same category.

Religious freedom does not mean one can violate state law or is above the law. Sharia law seeks to destroy our laws completely. Here is info from the above site that illustrates this:

This was in a Palestinian/Jordanian school book in 1998 and this sentiment is rampant today: "This religion (Islam) will destroy all other religions through the Islamic Jihad fighters."

Of course they cannot accomplish that without complete control of government. This also shows the attitude of Muslims toward terrorists. Killing innocents is applauded, especially if non-Muslim. It is a job, a way of life; it is their destiny as Muslims. Anything is ok if it promotes Islam. And Sharia law is a primary tool to accomplish that.

Terrorism

The documented and deadly 18th-century Wahhabi movement called all Muslims back to the last years of Mohammad, whereupon he practiced Jihad with unrestrained violent fury under Sharia law. This deeply affected the 35 nations of the Middle East, where 87% of them are now Muslim.

Muslims launched a confirmed 9,000-plus bloody attacks worldwide, including some on Israel, from 1981-2000, and the number seems to be growing dramatically since. The "moderates" have not been able (nor seemingly had the desire) to stop even one of these thousands of attacks, according to Randall Price, who spent years in Jerusalem ("Unholy War," pg. 178 and following).

In John Ankerberg and John Weldon's gem of a compact book, "Fast Facts on Islam," they quote Dr. Daniel Piper, who has made a long, careful study of

Islam, and the number of "radical terrorists," among them. They state that among the 1.3 billion Muslims worldwide, about 10% to 15% of them are hard-nosed terrorists, which equates to about 200 million extreme terrorists.

Yet all Muslims, "moderates" included, under Jihad and Sharia law, are required to fight and kill any and all non-Muslims, especially Jews and Christians, or they will be killed themselves, according to their own beliefs.

However peaceful, friendly and loving they may be or claim to be, their bloodthirsty religion has them encapsulated in its serpentine coils irrevocably. Muslims seem to enjoy the benefits in America nevertheless, even while knowingly or unknowingly betraying her.

"Moderate" Muslims

Now, let's consider the harsh reality of these "Moderate" Muslims. They are somewhat trapped, *ruefully* mourning the killings of 9/11 here in America, while celebrating openly elsewhere. Whether they are deceived or deceivers, willing or unwilling, they mask the real purpose of the Muslims, *Sharia law on all*, which includes the subjugation or killing of all non-Muslims. Is Islam really a *Religion of Peace*?

The Threat

We pass all of these warnings off as "Alarmist." We have begun to ignore the fulminations of Osama bin

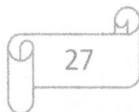

Laden. With surpassing insipidity, we are ignoring Iran and its obsessed leader, Ahmadinejad, who is working urgently to get nuclear weapons to wipe out Israel as soon as possible, unless Israel strikes first.

Israel says it will, if it must to survive. Any day they may have to strike—a preemptive strike. Never have we been nearer a nuclear holocaust.

Ahmadinejad is admired and cheered on by millions even though he is supposedly second in command in Iran. Ayatollah Khomeini, terror leader personified, is the first in command.

Al Qaeda began in Afghanistan, and now is "married" to Hezbollah. Osama bin Laden is the real founder, father and leader of this violent terrorist organization. He is a billionaire and finances it passionately.

Dirty Bombs

Paul L. Williams, in his revealing and alarming book, "The Day of Islam," published in 2007, declares unequivocally that "Dirty Bombs" are buried in some of our cities, waiting only for the Terrorist's signal for what they call the "American Hiroshima" to explode the bombs.

His research is massive and meticulous. He is convinced that America is doomed, as the full title of his book "The Day of Islam, The Annihilation of America and the Western World" indicates.

Williams gives dozens of names of terrorists and a brief summary of their activities in America and elsewhere. He also gives the name, terrorist record and history of the person that many regard as the most dangerous terrorist in the world, aside from Osama bin Laden. His name is Ayman al Zawahiri (pg. 24-25 in Williams' book).

Nuclear War

Ahmadinejad and Iran have, or soon will have, nuclear weapons, and it follows that they will try to find a way to use them to wipe out Israel. Their hatred of Israel and predictions for her destruction are a matter of public record.

Next, if not simultaneously, they will ardently seek to attack somnolent, appeasing America, with incredible fury and destruction causing the bloody death of millions. Why would we think otherwise? We dance blithely and watch soap operas while they plan disaster for us.

Investigative reporter and author Paul Williams, in his aforementioned book, "The Day of Islam," confirms that the terrorists refer to this upcoming attack as the "American Hiroshima."

Terrorist Training Camps

Muslim terrorists are now in the USA, and pouring in from both borders. Just on the outskirts of Hancock, New York, they have a 70 acre village called Islamberg, which is a Muslim training center for killing Jews and Christians, and all Americans.

For years it was unwittingly (I hope) funded by America, up to several million dollars annually, until the blind Sheik, who was trained there and trained others, was found to be involved in the World Trade Center bombing.

No matter, billionaire Osama bin Laden, and other Muslim sources foot the bill. Muslims from all over the world have been trained there. They are still being trained there to kill us and finish taking over America.

Farouq Mosque in Brooklyn, New York, has been training radical terrorists for years, whose sole aim is to murder us when it is time for the American Hiroshima. Intercepted phone conversations and papers found on dead or captured terrorists indicate the time is immediate, or very near.

Schools called Madrahas (also Madrassas or Madrassh) train children to hate and kill all non-Muslims, especially Jews and Christians, and provide potentially thousands of new suicide bombers. Many Muslim Mosques teach hatred of Jews and Christians and of all non-Muslims as well.

Action Steps

Step #1 – Reaching Muslims for Christ

Reaching Muslims for Christ is difficult, but is happening to some extent worldwide. Yet, although some Muslims have come to Christ and more will still, will this slow the freight train of disaster? Witnessing is

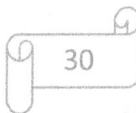

a worthwhile step certainly, but honestly I don't believe it will alter the threat.

I actually believe Muslims are similar to us when separated from Jihad peer pressure. They love their children, enjoy friends, make good neighbors, and possibly some have no real desire to kill or hurt anyone, even when pressured by their extremist peers, up to a point. But frankly, it is hard to get away from the notion that secretly the vast majority want Islamic rule.

And from research about and conversations with Muslims, I have learned sadly that they have no real *Savior* in their bleak and desolate religion because they reject Jesus, the only Savior for mankind, irrespective of religion. I care for Muslims, but fear greatly for their eternal destiny. Join with me and reach out to the few who might listen. This book is not based on hatred of them nor is it rooted in racism. We are all God's creation. He is a God of unity, not division. He is not willing that *any* should perish, including Muslims.

Step #2 – Electing Wise Leaders (Strict Constitutionalists) and Educating America

The problem is more than the Muslim threat. It is within us. We have turned away from God, in our homes, lives, schools, relationships, government and away from the doctrines our constitution was founded on. Unless we turn back we will collapse. Our land needs healing. We need wise, even Godly leaders, congressmen, senators, judges, school board members, parents and teachers to commit to righteous decisions.

And we need a media and leaders that will educate America about the threat. That is a primary reason for this book. We need preachers, newscasters, educators, and television and radio personnel to tell America the truth. We need citizens to stand up and be counted. <u>Politicians do pay attention to aroused voters.</u>

Step #3 – A Repentant Nation in Prayer

Let me share here what I feel is a *primary* hope for Muslims, Americans, and human beings worldwide. As always, it goes back to a Sovereign God and a submissive obedient nation. Grant Jeffrey says in his book, "The Signature of God," (Revised Edition) "The widespread agnosticism and atheism in government, mass media, universities and even theological schools has resulted in the moral collapse of our (American) society." Jeffrey says further that, "Philosopher Thomas Hobbes (1588-1679) . . . predicted the terrible results that would follow the widespread loss of faith in Christ in the United States."

Israel faced many trials, enemies and struggles in its long history as a nation, hundreds of years longer than America. When they were in trouble, and facing extinction, this is what God told them:

II Chronicles 7:14 (NIV) says, *"if my people, who are called by my name, will humble themselves and pray and seek my face and turn from their wicked ways, then I will hear from heaven, and I will forgive their sin and **will heal their land**."*

National Prayer

"A Prayer of Repentance"

This prayer has been attributed to Evangelist Billy Graham and to the late Paul Harvey of radio fame, ("The Rest of the Story") however Billy Graham did not use it and I rather doubt Paul Harvey did either.

The original version was written by Pastor Bob Russell and offered at a Governor's prayer breakfast in Frankfort, Kentucky, in 1995. It came to national prominence when it was revised by Rev. Joe Wright, Senior Pastor of the Central Christian Church in Wichita, and offered during an opening session, at the Kansas House of Representatives, in 1996.

It caused quite a stir. Afterwards, Rev. Joe Wright was quoted as saying, "I certainly did not mean to be offensive to individuals, but I don't apologize for the truth." He also said, "The problem I guess is that you're not supposed to get too specific when you talk about sin."

The prayer was read a month later by the Chaplain coordinator in the Nebraska legislature and again created a firestorm.

It was reportedly read in the Colorado legislature later that year. This should be America's National Prayer and it is easy to see why God has used it because it is certainly relevant today.

Floyd C. McElveen

National Prayer

We come before You today to ask Your Forgiveness and seek Your direction and guidance. We know Your Word says, "Woe to those who call evil good," but that's exactly what we have done. We have lost our Spiritual equilibrium and inverted our values.

* *We confess that; we have ridiculed the absolute truth of Your Word and called it pluralism;*
* *We have worshipped other gods and called it multiculturalism;*
* *We have endorsed perversion and called it an alternative lifestyle;*
* *We have exploited the poor and called it the lottery;*
* *We have neglected the needy and called it self-preservation;*
* *We have rewarded laziness and called it welfare;*
* *We have killed our unborn and called it choice;*
* *We have shot abortionists and called it justifiable;*
* *We have neglected to discipline our children and called it building self-esteem;*
* *We have abused power and called it political savvy;*
* *We have coveted our neighbor's possessions and called it ambition;*
* *We have polluted the air with profanity and pornography and called it freedom of expression;*
* *We have ridiculed the time-honored values of our forefathers and called it enlightenment.*

Search us, O God, and know our hearts today; try us and see if there be some wicked way in us; cleanse us from every sin and set us free. Guide and bless these men and women who have been sent here by the people of this (nation) and who have been ordained by You, to govern this great (nation). Grant them your wisdom to rule and may their decisions direct us to the center of Your Will.

I ask in the name of your Son, The Living Savior,
Jesus Christ.

In Conclusion

I am unaware of any other religious faith that won't peaceably co-exist with another. The key word is *"Peaceably."* Intimidation and terror are neither spiritual nor religious, but human evil run amuck.

Research this yourself. Read books and go online. Watch YouTube videos about "Hidden Jihad" and "Cultural Jihad." Converted Muslims will attest to the facts in this book and a lot more. Some will even state they were sent here to install Sharia law in insidious ways via "Cultural Jihad."

Each day there are news articles about killings, terror and intolerance by Islamic Nations. Muslims didn't suddenly become peaceful and tolerant upon arrival in America. Many have Muslim sponsors, funding and a hidden agenda. Their goal is to overthrow us whether peacefully or violently, they don't care. *They privately celebrate 9/11.*

Europe is being overrun and paying the cost. Sharia Law is gaining in momentum. Review recent court rulings in numerous states. These things are not just happening in 3rd world countries. They are occurring here and in Canada. In fact, Canada is further down this path than the United States.

So, now is the time America, please **wake up!**

References:

The Islamic Invasion by Dr. Robert Morey

Islam and Terrorism by Dr. Mark Gabriel

The Day of Islam, the Annihilation of America and the Western World by Dr. Paul L. Williams

Judgment Day by Dave Hunt

A Cup of Trembling by Dave Hunt

Unholy War by Dr. Randall Price

Behind the Veil Unmasking Islam by Dr. Abel el Schafi

Fast Facts on Islam by John Ankerberg and John Weldon

The Religion that is Raping America by Moody Adams

Deadly Deception by Moody Adams

The Islam Debate by Josh McDowell and John Gilchrist

The Last Jihad by Joel C. Rosenberg

The Signature of God—Revised by Grant Jeffery

YouTube.com

Crosswalk.com

And many quotes and summarizations throughout from *www.bibleprobe.com*

First Page: Bat Yeor - -
www.papillonsartpalace.com/cultuHre.htm

About the Author

Floyd C. McElveen has over 1.1 million books in print, in 8 or 9 languages, with 360,000 copies in Russia of *Evidence You Never Knew Existed* that is also published in Russia as *The Compelling Christ*, but most often under the title of *Facts You Need to Know About*.

One of McElveen's later books, published by Big Mac Publishers, is perhaps the crowning jewel, *So Send I You* (previously as *Unashamed, A Burning Passion to Share Christ*), which was endorsed by Dr. John Ankerberg, Dr. John Morris, the late Jerry Falwell, and others.

Other books include, *The Late Great American Church, The Beautiful Side Of Death, The Mormon Illusion*, God's *Word, Final, Infallible and Forever, Faith of an Atheist*, and *The Call of Alaska*.

McElveen wrote a book, and acted as producer of *Jesus Christ-Joseph Smith, a Search for the Truth*, on DVD, with over 500,000 copies distributed in English and thousands more translated into Spanish. The DVD is based on his book of same title.

"Mac" and late beautiful wife, Virginia

If this book has been an eye opener for you, informed you, or helped motivate you to get involved, please tell us and share this book with others. We have tried to make the cost of purchase very inexpensive. Buy a dozen and pass out to your leaders. It is also available as an eBook at Amazon, Barnes & Noble and Google.